99
QUOTES TO TRANSFORM

99 Sparks of Inspiration For 99 Days of Journaling

MANJUNATHA A R

NOTION PRESS

Published by
Notion Press Media Pvt Ltd,
#7, Red Cross Road,
Egmore, Chennai, Tamil Nadu 600008

Book title: 99 QUOTES TO TRANSFORM Volume-2
Subtitle: 99 Sparks of Inspiration For 99 Days of Journaling

ISBN XXX-X-XXXXXXX-X-X

First Impression April 2024
The moral right of the author has been asserted.
This edition is for sale worldwide.

Printed in India

Ordering Information
Quantity sales. Special discounts are available on quantity purchases by corporations, associations, and others. For details, contact the publisher at the address above.

NOTION PRESS

India. Singapore. Malaysia.

ISBN- XXX-X-XXXXXXX-X-X

Contents

Prologue

In this opening chapter, we embark on a journey delving into the wisdom and insights of stoics who have left a lasting impact on history. Through their words and experiences, we gain lessons and perspectives that hold the potential to shape our lives. As we explore the pages of this book, I invite you to open your mind and heart to the timeless guidance provided by these figures. Also, write about your experiences in those empty spaces and make them engaging to you. Get ready to feel inspired, motivated and empowered as we uncover the power of 99 quotes from stoics.

[*Globetrotting_Urban Saint*]
Place: Vijaynagar, Mysore
Date: 17/04/2024

***

"Failure isn't the end of the road; it's just a detour on the path to success."

- A.R

"Feedback is the compass that guides us towards improvement, leading us closer to our best selves."

- Globetrotting_Urban Saint

"The happiness of your life depends upon the quality of your thoughts."

- Marcus Aurelius

Watch out for your thoughts 24/7*365.

....

....

....

....

....

....

....

....

....

"Wealth consists not in having great possessions, but in having few wants."

- Epictetus

Less is More?

....

....

....

....

....

....

....

....

....

"The obstacle is the way."

- Marcus Aurelius

Know your obstacle if you are lost.

....

....

....

....

....

....

....

....

....

"Waste no more time arguing about what a good man should be. Be one."

- Marcus Aurelius

What matters is Actions, not words.

....
....
....
....
....
....
....
....
....

"The best revenge is not to be like your enemy."

- Marcus Aurelius

Work on yourself.

....

....

....

....

....

....

....

....

....

"It is not death that a man should fear, but he should fear never beginning to live."

- Marcus Aurelius

Live life, confront your fear and write down your fear.

....

....

....

....

....

....

....

....

....

"You have power over your mind - not outside events. Realize this, and you will find strength."

- René Descartes

All strength is within yourself, so don't look outside.

....
....
....
....
....
....
....
....
....

"The only way to do great work is to love what you do."

- Seneca

What do you love?

....

....

....

....

....

....

....

....

....

"Luck is what happens when preparation meets opportunity."

- Seneca

What are your preparations?

....

....

....

....

....

....

....

....

....

"He who fears death will never do anything worth of a man who is alive."

- Seneca

What do you want to do that is worth living?

....

....

....

....

....

....

....

....

....

"No person has the power to have everything they want, but it is in their power not to want what they don't have and to cheerfully put to good use what they do have."

- Seneca

Live, Don't complain?

....

....

....

....

....

....

"Don't explain your philosophy. Embody it."

- Epictetus

What is your philosophy for life?

....

....

....

....

....

....

....

....

....

"Caretake this moment. Immerse yourself in its particulars. Respond to this person, this challenge, this deed. Quit evasions. Stop giving yourself needless trouble. It is time to really live, to inhabit the situation you happen to be in now fully."

- Epictetus

"If you want to improve,
be content to be thought
foolish and stupid."

- Epictetus

Write down your limitations and doubts.

....

....

....

....

....

....

....

....

....

"First, say to yourself what you would be; then do what you have to do."

- Epictetus

Famous Tamasha Indian Movie Dialogue

"क्या है तेरे दिल के अंदर? चाहता क्या है तू? ? Bata, kya hai tere dil ke andar?🩶

It would be best if you found out who you are. It would help if you decided what it is that you want from life. No one can answer these questions for you. You have the power to write your own story; always remember that.

....

....

....

....

....

....

"Difficulties strengthen the mind, as labour does the body."

- Seneca

Do your labour daily with extreme sincerity towards your work.

....

....

....

....

....

....

....

....

....

"If a man knows not to which port he sails, no wind is favourable."

- Seneca

Fix Your Goal (Direction) Head towards your goal and show back to every other aspect of your journey.

....

....

....

....

....

....

....

....

....

"The soul becomes dyed with the colour of its thoughts."

- Marcus Aurelius

Always paint your life canvas with bright thoughts, and don't cloud your mind with darkness.

....

....

....

....

....

....

....

....

....

> "He who has a why to live can bear almost any how."

- Friedrich Nietzsche

Write your how and why now!

....

....

....

....

....

....

....

....

....

"We suffer more often in imagination than in reality."

- Seneca

Why suffer when you can Take Action?

....

....

....

....

....

....

....

....

....

"Freedom is the only worthy goal in life. It is won by disregarding things that lie beyond our control."

- Epictetus

List the things that need to be disregarded to get your freedom.

....

....

....

....

....

....

"Luck is a matter of preparation meeting opportunity."

- Seneca

Write the things you need to do daily to get yourself lucky.

....

....

....

....

....

....

....

....

....

"Wealth consists not in having great possessions, but in having few wants."

- Epictetus

Conquer yourself?

....

....

....

....

....

....

....

....

....

"The more we value things outside our control, the less control we have."

- Epictetus

Be true to yourself and do not engage in self-deception and things outside your control.

....

....

....

....

....

....

....

....

"The greatest blessing granted to mankind comes by way of madness, which is a divine gift."

- Socrates

Have you lost yourself in something you love and made about? Write down now.

....

....

....

....

....

....

"The wise man needs much but wants nothing; the fool needs nothing but wants everything."

- Seneca

Know your needs to minimize your wants.

....

....

....

....

....

....

"Fight fortune with thine own weapons, for she will give thee none which can be used against herself."

- Seneca

Fight fortune with your virtues.

....

....

....

....

....

....

"He is king who fears nothing and longs for nothing. Everyone may give himself the kingdom of noble thoughts. "

- Seneca

"Never can there be courage where there is not peace."

- Seneca

Do you agree?

....

....

....

....

....

....

....

....

....

"What we bear is not so important as how we bear it."

- Seneca

Process is important than result

....

....

....

....

....

....

....

....

....

....

"The good man bears calmly much that is not evil except to those that take it ill."

- Seneca

Let good man Rise within you!

....
....
....
....
....
....
....
....
....

"He yields to destiny and consoles himself by knowing that he is carried along with the universe."

- Seneca

Choose not! To yield to evil but to good.

....
....
....
....
....
....

"We become happy by not needing happiness."

- Seneca

Let's Count the blessings we have!

....

....

....

....

....

....

....

....

....

"Fortune conquers us unless she is conquered utterly."

- Seneca

That's why they say fortune favours bravery.

....

....

....

....

....

....

....

....

....

"He is free who arises above all injuries and finds all his joys within himself."

- Seneca

Endure, Adapt, overcome.

....

....

....

....

....

....

....

....

....

"There is nothing grand that is not also calm."

- Seneca

Become Calm, be grand.

....
....
....
....
....
....
....
....
....

"Wisdom shows her strength by her peace amid trouble, like an army encamped in safety in a hostile land."

- Seneca

Find your strength.

....

....

....

....

....

....

....

....

....

"In the upper air, there is neither cloud nor storm, and so in the lofty soul, there is always peace."

- Seneca

Do you agree?

....

....

....

....

....

....

....

....

....

"Peace of mind comes by meditating diligently over wise maxims, by doing our duty, and by setting our hearts on what is noble."

- Seneca

What's your duty?

....

....

....

....

....

....

....

"Fear and penitence for those who can neither rule nor obey their desires."

- Seneca

Do you feel?

....

....

....

....

....

....

....

....

....

"A very little can satisfy our necessities, but nothing our desires."

- Seneca

What do you prefer?

....

....

....

....

....

....

....

....

....

"He who longs to wear gold and purple is poor, not by fortune's fault, but by his own."

- Seneca

No longing for whatsoever.

....

....

....

....

....

....

....

....

....

"Nothing is so honourable as a great soul, but that soul is not great which can be shaken by either fear or grief."

- Seneca

Count your courage.

....
....
....
....
....
....
....
....
....

"The wise man will always know how to help the suffering. But sorrow prevents us from making distinctions, finding out what is useful, avoiding what is dangerous, and deciding what is just; therefore, he will not himself yield to sorrow. He will do everything that could be done by the sympathetic, but he will do it calmly and cheerfully."

- Seneca

"What is noble? To be able to bear adversity contentedly, taking whatever happens as if we had wished for it, as, indeed, we should have done since all things happen by the will of God. To weep or complain is to rebel."

- Seneca

"Which had you rather give up--yourself or some of your troubles?"

- Seneca

Give up your.

....

....

....

....

....

....

....

....

....

"He has reached the height of wisdom who knows what to rejoice in and does not place his happiness in another's power."

- Seneca

Choose wisely.

....

....

....

....

....

....

....

"He has reached the supreme good who is never sad or excited by hope but keeps an even and happy frame of mind by day and night."

- Seneca

Always have room for good temperament.

....

....

....

....

....

"The wise man's joy is woven so well as not to be broken by any accident."

- Seneca

Have you ever broken?

....

....

....

....

....

....

....

....

....

"Take care not to make your pain greater by your complaints. If you will say, 'It is nothing,' or, at least, 'It is slight, and about to cease,' you will make it what you think it."

- Seneca

What's your thought?

....

....

....

"What is really evil? To yield to what is called so and give up our liberty, which ought to be kept at every cost. Farewell, freedom, if we do not scorn everything that would enslave us!"

- Seneca

Do not Yield; Do it right now.

....

....

....

"The grandest of empires is to rule one's self."

- Seneca

What do you want to lift?

....
....
....
....
....
....
....
....
....

"Philosophy will give us the greatest of blessings--freedom from regret."

- Seneca

philosophy
/fɪˈlɒsəfi/

a theory or attitude that acts as a guiding principle for

behaviour?

....

....

....

....

....

....

....

....

....

"This is grand, to act always like the same man."

- Seneca

Live Grand?

....
....
....
....
....
....
....
....

"My country is wherever I am happy, and that depends on the man, not the place."

- Seneca

That's how power works: take responsibility.

....

....

....

....

....

....

....

....

....

"Who has the most? He who desires least."

- Seneca

Are you happy with what you have?

....

....

....

....

....

....

....

....

....

"Sickness is a hindrance to the body, but not to the will, unless that yields."

- Epictetus

Goodwill yield to virtues, not to wises?

....

....

....

....

....

....

....

....

....

"If a little oil be spilt, or a little wine was stolen, say to yourself, 'This is the price of tranquillity and peace; nothing is to be had without cost."

- Epictetus

Do you understand?

....

....

....

....

....

....

....

....

"Everything has two handles and can be carried by one of them but not by the other."

- Epictetus

One ship, one captain?

....
....
....
....
....
....
....
....
....

"He who has learned that prosperity and peace consist in not missing what we seek, or suffering what we shun, keeps down his desires, and shuns only what he can avoid."

- Epictetus

Live, don't just survive?

....

....

....

"Whoever shuns, or desires, what is not in his own power, cannot be either faithful or free."

- Epictetus

Do it, don't shun.

....

....

....

....

....

....

....

....

....

"Why should I care what happens while my soul is above it?"

— Epictetus

Know what is inside you and believe?

....

....

....

....

....

....

....

....

....

"This is education, to learn to wish that things should happen as they do."

- Epictetus

Face as it comes, not as you wish it.????

....

....

....

....

....

....

....

....

....

"The essence of good and evil lies in the direction of the will, for which all outward things are means to help it reach its own evil or good."

- Epictetus

What's your aspiration?

....

....

....

....

....

....

"If you choose to keep your will in harmony with nature, you are safe and free from care."

- Epictetus

Good will hunting.

....
....
....
....
....
....
....
....
....

"Show me someone who is sick, in danger, disgraced, dying, but yet happy. Show him, for I long to see a Stoic!"

- Epictetus

Let's create stoicism within us.

....
....
....
....
....
....
....
....
....

"The child who tries to take too many nuts and figs out of a jar with a narrow mouth so that his hand is caught must drop some to get out the rest. Have but few wants, and they will be supplied."

- Epictetus

Less is more?

....

....

....

"He bears a fever well who blames neither God nor man, and does not trouble himself about what may happen, but awaits death nobly."

- Epictetus

Find your pain and endure; that's how strong will is created.

....

....

....

"If you see anybody wail and complain, call him a slave, though he is clad in purple."

- Epictetus

Don't be that slave?

....

....

....

....

....

....

....

....

....

"Freedom is not gained by satisfying, but by restraining our desires."

- Epictetus

Focus on enduring pain, not on pleasure?

....

....

....

....

....

....

....

....

"Of what use is your reading if it does not give you peace?"

- Epictetus

Peace in between pages of books.

....

....

....

....

....

....

....

....

....

"Not only ambition and avarice, but even desire of ease, of quiet, of travel, or of learning, may make us base and take away our liberty."

- Epictetus

Never cling; what are you clinging to?

....

....

....

....

....

....

"Rejoice in what you have, and like whatever time brings."

- Epictetus

Go with the flow, but sail well?

....
....
....
....
....
....
....
....

"Wherever I go, it will be well with me, as it has been here, and on account not of the place, but of the principles which I shall carry away with me. They are all my property, and they will be all I shall need, wherever I may be."

- Aristotle.

"It is not poverty, but covetousness, that causes sorrow. It is not wealth, but philosophy, that gives security."

- Epictetus

Write your philosophy.

....

....

....

....

....

....

"Make your daily food
not of expense and
trouble but of frugality
and joy."

- Epictetus

Write your values and the integrity you hold.

....

....

....

....

....

....

....

....

....

"Time delivers fools
from grief and reason-
wise men."

- Epictetus

Time tests.

....
....
....
....
....
....
....
....
....

"He is wise who rejoices in what he has and does not grieve for what he has not."

- Epictetus

Write your 10% and 90% Rule.

....
....
....
....
....
....
....
....
....

"Fortify thyself in contentment, for this is a fortress which cannot be taken easily."

- Epictetus

Ask Now contentment in your Action!

....

....

....

....

....

....

....

....

....

"How easy to drive away every thought that is troublesome or unfriendly and be at peace at once."

- Marcus Aurelius

Break The CAGE of Thoughts Which Limits You?

....

....

....

....

....

....

....

"Nothing comes upon any man which he is not formed to bear."

- Marcus Aurelius

Do you know the virtues that decide your destiny?

....

....

....

....

....

....

....

....

....

"The mind turns every obstacle into an aid."

- Marcus Aurelius

Your mind is your friend and your foe.

....

....

....

....

....

....

....

....

....

"Nothing that happens injures me unless I take it as an evil, and it is in my power not to take it so."

- Marcus Aurelius

Take extreme accountability.

"Always remember that very little is needed for living a happy life."

- Marcus Aurelius

Work within yourself?

....

....

....

....

....

....

....

....

....

"Whatever happens is an opportunity for acting reasonable and kindly; in short, becomingly, toward either God or man."

- Marcus Aurelius

What are you Looking at?

....

....

....

"Is it not better to use what thou hast, like a free man, than to long, like a slave, for what is not in thy power?"

- Marcus Aurelius

What are you creating out of your life slave or master?

....

....

....

"Man becomes better and nobler by making the right use of all that comes to pass."

- Marcus Aurelius

Define everything that comes to you.

....

....

....

....

....

....

"The soul has the power to live most happily if she will not be anxious about what is unimportant."

- Marcus Aurelius

Delegate, detach, and delete what is unimportant.

....

....

....

....

....

....

"O, Father, courage does not consist in fearing to live, but in resisting great evils, and not giving way; for to die on account of them is to be conquered."

- Seneca

Conquer your fear?

....

....

....

"It is to make us noble that God gives us such opportunities of growth in strength and courage as can be found only in adversity."

- Seneca

Is adversity an advance to the next level?

....

....

....

....

....

....

"Calamity is an opportunity for courage."

- Seneca

What is behind you, and what bestows you courage?

....
....
....
....
....
....
....
....
....

"That courage is most to be relied on, which reflects long, moves slowly, and carries out what has been settled deliberately."

- Seneca

Do you agree?

....
....
....
....
....
....

"What is noble? A soul brave and steadfast under adversity; not only indifferent, but hostile to dissipation- neither seeking nor flying danger; knowing how to make a fortune instead of waiting for her; meeting all her changes calmly, and being never overcome either by her tempests or by her splendours."

- Seneca

"It is better to grow braver than more learned, but neither can be done without the other."

- Seneca

What's in your heart?

....
....
....
....
....
....
....
....
....

"Throw away all anxiety about life, and so make it pleasant."

- Seneca

What's Your Plan of Action?

....

....

....

....

....

....

....

....

....

"A brave and wise man should not flee from life."

- Seneca

What's your sacrifice for your greatness?

....

....

....

....

....

....

....

....

....

"There is no happiness where there is any fear."

- Seneca

Do you know your fear?

....

....

....

....

....

....

....

....

....

"True courage will avoid danger, but not fear it."

- Seneca

What's your plan to face danger?

....

....

....

....

....

....

....

....

....

"Courage is careful to preserve itself and ready to endure what is evil in appearance only."

- Seneca

Are you Ready To RISE with courage?

....

....

....

....

....

....

Epilogue

As we come to the end of our expedition, we reflect on the influence of the words and wisdom shared by stoic individuals throughout history. Each quote has acted as a guiding light illuminating our path towards growth and transformation. As you close this book, may you carry with you the lessons absorbed and insights gained, using them as tools to navigate life's obstacles and pursue your aspirations with unwavering dedication. Remember that each one of us holds within us the power to transform, waiting for us to tap into it through the wisdom passed down by those who preceded us. Embrace what lies ahead with confidence, knowing that you possess the strength and resilience needed to conquer any challenge and achieve greatness.

We will meet in Volume 3…………..

With appreciation and optimism

[*Globetrotting_ Urban Saint*]

***

VOL - 1
#10 Best Mindsets
For Self Improvement
MINDSET
MATTERS
MANJUNATHA A.R

AR 003*

VOL - 1
99
Quotes
to
transform
"99 Sparks of Inspiration
For 99 Days of Journaling"
MANJUNATHA A R

AR 004*

Share Your Thoughts

manjunatha_a.r

Manjunatha A.R

Manjunatha A R

Manjunatha_A_R

manjunatha_a_r

Manjunatha_AR

99 days Challenge

Are you ready for a transformative journey? If yes, then accept the 99-day challenge by starting to write this journal today.

This collection of 99 thought-provoking quotes is designed to ignite your imagination and inspire personal growth. The quotes and wisdom from notable stoics who have left an indelible mark on history offer timeless guidance for personal development. Every day, reflect on a new quote and let its wisdom permeate your thoughts and actions. Through introspection and application, you'll discover new depths within yourself and unlock your potential for profound transformation. So, embrace the challenge today and let the journey begin.

***

Note